D1649406

Eavesdropping
on
Adolph Hitler

Copyright © 2013 Ian Mayo-Smith
All rights reserved. No part of this publication may be reproduced, distrib-
uted, stored in a retrieval system, or transmitted, in any form or by any
means, electronic, mechanical, photocopying, recording or otherwise without the
written prior permission of the publisher, except in the case of brief quota-
tions embodied in critical reviews and certain other non-commercial uses per-
mitted by copyright law. For permission requests write to the publisher
Four Pillars Media Group at P.O.Box 499, Meriden, CT 06450

Dedicated to all my colleagues and friends who took part in any
way in the breaking of enemy codes and ciphers at Bletchley Park
and its outstations during World War II. It still amazes me how
much fun and satisfaction we got from doing it, this wonderful
band of brothers and sisters.

ISBN: 978-0-9857093-2-7
Library of Congress Control Number: 2012952852

Cover design by Marilyn Penrod.

Eavesdropping
on
Adolph Hitler

Deciphering the daily
messages in the Tunny cipher

A Bletchley Park veteran remembers

Ian Mayo-Smith

Four Pillars Media Group

Acknowledgments

The author acknowledges with grateful thanks the people who helped him to revive old memories from seven decades ago and put together this short memoir of life as a member of the Testery at Betchley Park. It was Kelsey Griffin at BP who first encouraged him to undertake this task. His conversations with former Captain Jerry Roberts helped to revive old memories. Ann Winfield gave generously of her time in improving Ian's original writings with her careful editing. Marilyn Penrod contributed the evocative cover. But most of all it was my wife, Krishna Sondhi, a former publisher herself, who kept my nose to the grindstone giving me little peace until the MS was ready to go to the printer. She also provided all the photographic illustrations except for the black and white photo on page vi. My colleagues at Four Pillars Media Group, Brian Walsh, Maura Satchell and Catherine Wyatt-Morley also consistently gave their support and advice wherever and whenever it was needed.

The Greatest Secret of World War II

Never heard of the cipher breaking work at Bletchley Park?
Read on

If you live in Britain and listen to the BBC you have probably heard all about Bletchley Park and the work that was done there during World War II. If so, you can skip this note and go on to reading the book.

If however you live in the United States or some other part of the English-speaking world you may not have heard about the biggest World War II secret, known as Bletchley Park. The truth is that Bletchley Park was the centre of major British Intelligence activities during World War II. This short book is about one part of those activities, the code breaking.

You may perhaps have seen the film *Enigma* which was about one aspect of this code breaking. It was a very important part of the work done there but the film gave a misleading impression of Bletchley. It showed it as being a rather unhappy place where people worked in grim earnestness and didn't seem to be getting much fun out of life. The breaking of the version of Enigma used by the German Navy was of great importance because it enabled the Allied navies to know the whereabouts of German submarines which were attacking the ships bringing supplies across the Atlantic to Britain, and the people responsible were far from being grim and dull. They were a very creative and lively group of people.

But even if you have heard about Enigma, I would guess that you have not heard about another much more complex machine cipher known as Tunny. This was the cipher used by Hitler himself and his top commanders to communicate with each other. Those of us who worked on the deciphering of messages in Tunny were not allowed to talk about it for many decades. We had been sworn to silence and we kept our promise. In fact it was not until the middle 1980s that the ban which kept us silent was lifted and we were at last permitted to speak and to write about our wartime work.

Most people are under the impression that the first electronic computer was designed and built in the United States. That is not so. The first electronic computers were already in use at Bletchley Park and they were used to complete one part of the process of deciphering the Tunny cipher.

The American Present Dwight Eisenhower,

when he was Supreme Commander of the Allied Forces in Europe, went on record, saying that the information he received which came from Bletchley Park (much of it from decrypts of messages sent in Tunny) helped shorten the war by many months and saved hundreds of thousands of lives. The work we did certainly played an important role in the Allied victory.

This book is the personal memoir of someone who as a young soldier was part of the group that deciphered Tunny. Looking back I can see what a privilege it was to have been part of it There are not many of us left who can talk or write about it first hand.

I hope you will enjoy reading about what it was like to be part of that group.

Two happy members of the Sergeants Mess at Bletchley on a borrowed motorbike.
Sgt Joan Chandler (later Allander) and Staff Sgt Ian Mayo-Smith.

Contents

Notes

Army ranks and abbreviations.

W.O.I. A Warrant Officer Class One holds the highest non-commissioned rank in the British army. Depending on which branch of the army they are in they may hold the title of Regimental Sergeant Major. (RSM) or Staff Sergeant Major (SSM). A W.O. I wears the Royal Coat of Arms on the sleeve of his or her uniform.

W.O.II. A Warrant Officer Class Two holds the next highest rank and may be designated a Company Sergeant Major (CSM), Staff Quarter Master Sergeant (SQMS) or Regimental Quarter Master Sergeant (RQMS). A W.O. II wears a crown surrounded by a wreath on the sleeve of his or her uniform.

A soldier with three chevrons with a crown above them on his arm is a **Staff Sergeant** (SSgt). This rank is immediately below that of W.O. II and above that of Sergeant.

German Names

To Umlaut or not to Umlaut. In German the vowels A, O and U often have their pronunciation modified by placing an umlaut (two dots) above them. When words containing these modified vowels are transcribed into English the custom is normally to add an E to the vowels. So that Dr Gobbels (with an umlaut over the O) becomes Dr Goebbels and the Fuhrer (umlaut over the U) becomes the Fuehrer. I am glad that this convention exists as the keyboard on which this book was written contains no provision for umlauts!

How I Got to Bletchley Park

At 88 I can remember what I was doing at the age of 18, 70 years ago, more clearly than I can remember where I put my reading glasses down ten minutes ago. I can remember my first year at Cambridge. I went up to Clare College at the age of 17, so I suppose I was fairly bright. Yes, I definitely must have been fairly bright, as I can also remember during that same year going to the army recruiting office in Holloway Road in a poor part of London to volunteer. I was given the usual medical exam and the multipage army intelligence test. I caused some astonishment as I scored 100 per cent. "You've seen this before, haven't you?" the Segreant in charge asked, "No, Sergeant, I've never seen it before." "You must have. You got all the answers right" he said with astonishment. Consternation. I guess after that I was a marked man.

Anyway I was enrolled as a private in the Queen's Royal Regiment and told to go back to Cambridge. They said that I would be called to active duty after the end of the academic year. So I returned to continue my studies in French and German. I even did an intensive workshop in German during the vacation, though I am not quite sure now whether that was because I was so keen to perfect my knowledge of the language or whether it was because some rather attractive girls had also signed up for it. On the workshop I remember that I had to take the part of a German business man with a lisp when we did a read through of the play "Im Weissen Roessl" (The White Horse Inn.) It was enough of a struggle reading through the script and trying to do it with an impeccable German accent but to do it with a lisp – that was a bit too much.

I had joined the Cambridge University Senior Training Corps (CUSTC) and went for military training one or more times a week. I gained the training corps Certificate A and then stayed on at the end of term for an extended period doing full time military training for a Certificate B, so by the time the call came for me to report for duty I had already completed the training and obtained the qualifications that would, before the war, have entitled a Cambridge graduate to receive a commission with six months seniority over a Sandhurst graduate.

I was sent to Norton Barracks, Worcester, for basic army training. It was really an almost complete waste of time as I had already completed much more advanced training in the CUSTC, but it did give me my first taste of dealing on equal terms with young men of my own age who came from backgrounds quite different from the comfortable upper middle class background that I had. It also gave me my first understanding of the social standings of different ranks in the armed forces. For example the Regimental Sergeant Major (RSM) had to salute a Second Lieutenant, because the latter held the King's Commission whereas the RSM was a Warrant Officer. On the other hand all the subalterns (Lieutenants and Second Lieutenants) had to attend a weekly Subalterns Parade where they were drilled by the RSM, who was not slow in showering scorn on those young officers who did not come up to his requirements. We private soldiers, being the lowest form of life that walked the earth, used to watch as the RSM shouted at some Lieutenant that he was "a dozy idle gentleman." I also remember the physical training instructor, Sergeant Roly Jenkins, a prominent cricketer who played county cricket for Worcestershire.

I cannot say that I found being a private soldier a great hardship. After all I had been a boarder at Aldenham School, the English public school founded by Queen Elizabeth I's brewer. (For the benefit of non-English readers I should explain that an English "public school" is in fact an elite private boarding school, usually one that had been founded at least a century or more ago.) At Aldenham there weren't officers but there were masters, who fulfilled much the same function. Instead of NCOs (non-commissioned officers, i.e corporals and sergeants and such) there were praeposstors. In most other schools they were called prefects.) The school discipline was very similar to army discipline, but the army food was better than the school food.

Having completed the basic training ("boot camp" if you are American) I was sent to the Intelligence Corps depot for further training. The I Corps depot was located in the largest palace in Britain, Wentworth Woodhouse, the ancestral home of the Earls Fitzwilliam. We private soldiers were quartered in the stables. All the trainees received the same training to start with. In addition to such subjects as map reading, there were more exciting topics such as interrogation techniques, in which (though this would probably be denied by the Ministry of Defence) we were taught how to encourage captured enemies to talk by employing such elementary torture methods as holding a lightened match under the sole of one of the unfortunate fellow's feet and other tricks not endorsed by the Geneva convention. We were taught how to break open safes without damaging the contents inside them. The Sergeant Instructor referred to this session as "postwar careers." Rumour had it that in civvy street he had been a professional burglar.

The majority of the trainees were destined to become Field Security Personnel (FSP, often referred to as Field Security Police) and after completing this part of the course they were taught motor bike riding skills which they would need for their work in the field. But I was not destined to join the FSP and the rest of my training was to take place elsewhere.

One day, I was instructed to get all my kit together, including my rifle, and prepare for a transfer. I was then given a railway warrant to Bradford with instructions to report to 1, Albany Road, in that city. I set off with the heavy load of my steel helmet, my gasmask, and my backpack with all my worldly belongings on my back and carrying my rifle. I got on the train at Rotherham. My memories of the rail journey are rather vague except for one incident which sticks out vividly in my mind. At some point I had to change trains to go on another line to Bradford. In the railway compartment that I got into there was an RAF Wing Commander and his wife. When I got off the train at the station where I had to change trains, I was walking along the platform to go to the platform for my connection when I heard a female voice shouting "Soldier, soldier!" I turned round. It was the wife of the Wing Commander and she was carrying my rifle. "Soldier, you forgot your gun." She handed me my rifle and hurried back to rejoin her husband, as I blurted out my thanks. She had saved me from committing the ultimate crime for a soldier, that of losing my weapon. I will be eternally grateful to that lady. She probably saved me from spending the rest of the war in a military prison. What had happened was that when I had put all my belongings, backpack, tin hat, gasmask and rifle up on the luggage rack, my rifle had gone right to the back of the rack and when I put on the pack, gas mask, and tin hat I had not noticed my rifle. Fully encumbered as I was, I thought I had everything. Thank God, for the keen eyes of the Wing Commander and/or his wife. They had seen it and she rushed out to hand it to me. A guardian angel, if ever there was one.

Finally I did get to the Bradford railway station and I got off the train with all my gear intact and I went to the office of the Railway Transport Officer (RTO) to ask for directions. He looked at my movement order and scratched his head. "This is a very strange order," he said. "We don't normally get orders for someone to report to a postal address, but to a military unit. I don't know of any military unit at this address." He then phoned the local postmaster and asked him where Albany Road was. The postmaster assured him there was no such road in Bradford. "Look here," he said, "There must be some mistake. I'll send a signal to your unit to find out what's happened. Meanwhile I'll send you to the local barracks where you can spend the night. Then report back to me tomorrow morning."

The next day, when I reported, he told me there had been a mistake, I should have been sent to 1, Albany Road Bedford, not Bradford. He gave me a new railway warrant and I was on my way.

1, Albany Road turned out to be an unremarkable private house in a quiet street. There was no sign outside it to indicate that it housed any kind of military establishment, but inside it was the army's cipher breaking (or cryptanalysis) training school. It was staffed by a Major, a Captain, a Staff Quarter Master Sergeant (SQMS or Warrant Officer Class II) and a Sergeant. SQMS Peddler and Sergeant Hatch were both from the Royal Army Service Corps and were in charge of all administrative arrangements, including arranging our accommodation with various families in the town.

I was extremely fortunate as with three others I was billeted with a lady named Mrs Judge, a widow, who had for many years with her husband kept a pub. Remarkably both she and her late husband had been teetotallers themselves. She lived in the house with her two stepdaughters. She really looked after our comfort and fed us very well. We could not have had a better landlady. Mind you we in turn were expected to behave like gentlemen. We never tried to date her attractive younger step-daughter Beryl, who was about the same age as we were. She was definitely off limits to us, although perfectly friendly.

For a brief while the four of us were joined by a Corporal from the RAF who was a body builder. With Mrs Judge's permission he brought his "wife" to join him one weekend. When Mrs Judge learned from his RAF unit that he was not married, he was immediately kicked out.

Some of the others attending the course were not nearly so lucky as the four of us. Two of them were billeted on a family, two of whose members were prostitutes and where my two fellow trainees were regarded as very unwelcome guests.

Our instructors in cryptanalysis were Major Masters of the Royal Signals and a Captain from the Intelligence Corps, whose name, if I remember rightly, was Cheadle or Cheatham. We were provided with work books which explained the various types of ciphers and included a series of exercises which we had to do.

. The two officers would frequently check to see how we were getting on. After several weeks a group of about half a dozen of us were considered ready to be sent to Bletchley Park to work in the Testery, named after its head, Major Ralph Tester.

By this time we had all except one been transferred to the Intelligence Corps and were still private soldiers. The exception was W.O.II Carney of the Royal Signals Corps.

We took the train from Bedford to Bletchley Junction. But this time we were not encumbered with rifles. We had handed them in at Bedford and I personally was only too happy not to see mine ever again. At Bletchley Junction, Carney, as the senior person in the group, formed us into a squad and marched us to the army camp adjacent to

Bletchley Park, which was to be our home for the next two years.

The author standing in front of the mansion at Bletchley Park as it is today.
It is now an extremely interesting museum.

Tunny and the Lorenz Machine

If those of us who came to work in the Testery
after our training in Bedford thought we knew everything
worth knowing about ciphers, we were in for a rude awaken-
ing. First we had to learn a new alphabet because the Tunny
cipher was based on "teleprinter language," unlike ciphers
such as Enigma which were based on the Morse code. At that
time there were 32 characters in the language of teleprinters
and that number could be doubled, for if you wrote
teleprintese in upper case, you got numbers and punctuation
marks as opposed to letters.

Teleprinters used the Baudot code. (See the diagram
below.) To tell the truth I did not know that was what it was
called until I read Tony Sale's excellent article on the Tunny
cipher on the internet from which the illustration below was
taken. (You can find the article on Google.)

We had never heard of the "Tunny" cipher or the Lorenz machine on which the teleprinter messages were enciphered. We just called it "Tunny" or sometimes just "Fish." It was used to carry messages between the German Supreme Command in Berlin and the High Commands in all the countries in Europe that were under German domination. It was used by the Fuehrer himself and some times we found a message signed by Goebbels, but most came from the top military men.

Each link was known by the name of a different fish. About the only one I can remember now is "Bream" which was the name that had been given to the link between Berlin and Rome. The messages were relayed over the air electronically from teleprinter to teleprinter.

As in all substitution ciphers the clear text was changed by superimposing on it a key. The more complicated the key the more difficult it was to break the cipher. The key used in Tunny was very complicated indeed.

In this day and age when virtually everyone has access to technology that enables people to send messages, encrypted or not, from any place in the world to any other place in the world by email, it is hard to realize that the technology involved in the Tunny cipher was the cutting edge technology of the time.

Teleprinters sent messages electronically by transmitting a stream of letters in the form of impulses sent in groups of five. In effect this meant sending out five separate streams simultaneously because (as indicated in the chart above) each character was composed of five parts. Each one of the five parts could either indicate a charge or the absence of a charge. On a teleprinter tape this would appear as holes or no holes. (In our working on the cipher we showed holes as crosses (X) and no holes as dots (.) The letter A was represented by two holes (XX) followed by three blanks(...). M was the exact opposite of A and consisted of three blanks followed by two holes. (See the chart above.) If you imposed a key letter M on the clear letter A the result was a letter with five holes, since when an X was imposed on a dot or vice versa, the result was an X but if a dot was imposed on another dot or an X was imposed on another X the result was a dot. In other words when like was imposed on like the result was always a dot but when unlikes were imposed on each other the result was always an X. An X always took precedence over a dot. So if an A was added to a C you got an F, and a G plus an H gave you a C. The idea was simple enough. If you knew what the key letter was you could tell what the clear message letter was, but the whole difficulty in breaking any substitution cipher is in finding out what the key letters are and how they are formed.

The Lorenz machine turned out the key and added it to the clear language in a very complex manner, for there was not just one set of keys but two and these were added together before they were added to the text. Moreover one set of keys was made to stutter by another set of keys so that the second key stream came out in a stuttering fashion.

The first set of keys, known to us as the Chi keys was created by five sets of wheels each of which created one of the five strands of dots and crosses making up the keys. The first wheel was 23 spaces long, the second 26, the third 29. The fourth 31, and the fifth 41. This meant that the key

12

would not repeat itself until it had completed a run of 22,041,682 cycles. You would think that this would make it almost impossible to work out the key and decipher the hidden clear message. And since each message would be started with the wheels in a different position you had an almost unbreakable cipher. But the maker of the Lorenz machine was not satisfied with creating an almost unbreakable cipher; he was determined to make a *completely* unbreakable cipher. So he added a second set of keys that would be superimposed on the first set. This second set of keys was referred to as the Psi keys and they also consisted of five wheels, the first wheel was of a length of 43, the second of 47, the third of 51, the fourth of 53 and the fifth of 59. This yields a total of 322,303,017 cycles. Now put the two keys together and you have to have a run of 22,041,682 x 322,303,017 before the key will begin to repeat itself. My desktop calculator cannot manage to calculate that number but it is, well, colossal. Surely no one could ever break such a cipher. But the designers of the Lorenz machines were still not satisfied, so just to make life more difficult for code breakers they added two more keys, known as the motor keys, to their design. One was 61 spaces long and the other 37 which gives you a total of a mere 2257. But this stream was used differently from the Chi and Psi keys; it was used to cause the Psi keys to stutter. So if the Psi keys had been left alone they might have produced a string of letters that read in part like this AJRBOUCRMKWC, but the effect of these two additional keys was to make it come out something like this AAJJRBOUUUCRMKKKWCC.

Incredible as it might seem, the geniuses and near

geniuses at Bletchley, such as Brigadier John Tiltman and Bill Tutte, had not only managed to figure out the structure of the Tunny cipher but were even able to decipher it, though it was a slow and painstaking business. They were helped in this by the Germans who one time made the dreadful mistake of sending two messages with almost the same text and their machines set up in exactly the same way, i.e. with exactly the same key settings each time. They also made another mistake that helped in breaking the cipher. In the early days they prefaced each transmission with a list of twelve double digit figures. The purpose of this was to tell the operator at the other end how to set up his machine. But to the cipher breakers they indicated that somehow twelve keys were involved.

If this effort at explaining the working of the Lorenz cipher has left the reader more confused than informed, I apologize and would suggest that you Google the excellent article on the subject by the late Tony Sale, to which I referred on page 17.

The Testery

As mentioned earlier, when our train got to Bletchley Junction, we marched the short distance to the military camp. After we were settled in we were issued security passes and taken into the Park itself and to the particular building where the Testery was situated. It was there we were introduced to the Tunny cipher, a cipher more complex than anything we had dreamed of,

The Testery was busy 24 hours each day every day of the year so the work was split into three shifts. Each shift was under one of the three shift leaders, and each shift was made up of three teams. These were the breakers who made the first short break into the encrypted message; the setters who extended that break until the keys for the message could all be set; and the typists who typed in the nonsense of the encrypted message and were rewarded by seeing clear language in German coming out of the printer.

We were all allocated to work as a setters. I was made a member of Captain Peter Ericsson's shift.

The next few weeks were spent in learning our job in

the Testery, getting familiar with the camp, and getting used to the ways of Bletchley Park. For example, the head of the Military Wing of the Park's operation, Brigadier John Tiltman, had decreed that there would be no saluting within the Park. In fact little regard was paid to military rank at all. Tiltman saw us all as colleagues working on a vital project. As well as the army personnel in the Testery there was a small number of civilians.

The first army cryptographers working on Tunny were all commissioned and by the time I got there they had reached the rank of Captain. Some of those who came a little later, like Peter Benenson were needed to start work immediately. To have sent them for officer training would have taken time, and besides that they might not have passed all aspects of the tests that prospective officers had to pass before being granted commissions. To get around this difficulty they were given promotion to Warrant Officer, Class One (W.O.I), the highest non-commissioned rank.

There was only one instance that I know of when this collegial equality regardless of rank caused a problem. This was when a Major, who shall remain nameless, was posted to the Testery. In civilian life he had worked for Collins, the publishers. As a major he was of the same rank as Major Ralph Tester after whom the section was named, and he was clearly not happy to be in a situation where officers and other ranks called each other by their first names and where rank had little to do with the work to which one was assigned. After a short while he disappeared and no doubt found a posting more to his liking.

We newcomers to the Testery got to know the people

we worked with and we started to get to know the town where we were situated. We also had to get used to the shift system. The day shift went from 9 am to 4 pm; the evening shift went from 4 pm until midnight. The night shift was the longest shift lasting from midnight until 9 am the next day. After a week on the night shift, coming off duty at 9 am, you then started on the evening shift, so you did not have to go back to work until 4 pm the next day, giving you a 31 hour break. After the week of working the evening shift you then went on the day shift.

Before we were able to work efficiently as members of the team of Setters, there were things we had to learn and to internalize completely so that we did not have to think about them. First there was the Baudot alphabet used by teleprinters.

This entailed being able to know how to add two letters together to get a third letter, as described in the previous chapter. Then we had to become familiar with the structure of the five keys that made up the Tunny cipher, the five Chi keys, the five Psi keys and the two motor keys. To my surprise it only took a very short time, about a week, I think, for all this to become second nature to us. The team of Setters on Peter Ericsson's shift was headed by a Captain, but here my memory breaks down as I cannot remember either his name or his appearance. The rest of the team consisted of Other Ranks (Enlisted Men in American parlance.)

The first part of the breaking of a Tunny enciphered message took place in our sister section, the Newmanry, headed by the mathematician Max Newman. With the help of the world's first electronic computer, Colossus, operated by Wrens (members of the Women's Royal Naval Service) under the guidance of mathematicians and cryptographers, the first set of five keys, the Chi keys, were stripped from the enciphered message. The resultant "de-chis" were passed to the Testery, where they went through three more processes, so that all twelve of the keys could be uncovered. The first step in uncovering the remaining seven keys (the Psi keys and the motor keys) was carried out by the Breakers. These were the most highly skilled and experienced of the cryptographers in the Testery and their job was to identify a stretch of about 30 to 50 letters in plain text to reveal the patterns of the keys underneath. They did this by learning to recognize certain patterns in the text of the de-chis that resulted from the use of certain terms and phrases that occurred frequently in the transmissions. For example the German phrase, "Bitte wiederholen Sie" (please repeat) was one such phrase. Words like "Gesellschaft" and all the other words ending in "schaft" could also be helpful. Some of the punctuation marks, for example "9++MA889" indicating the end of a sentence gave very distinctive patterns.

An attempt was made to automate the job of the Breakers. A machine had been designed and made in the United States. You could feed a German phrase into the machine and it would "drag" it through a de-chi. With luck it would find a place where the German phrase showed a match with the text of the de-chi that would also match with the Psi keys. This would create a break in exactly the same way that the Breakers did manually. The machine arrived from the United States accompanied by American army Sergeant Collins who was to be its operator. The idea behind the machine was sound but its success was very limited. Unfortunately it lacked one thing that the human breakers had and that was intuition.

After the initial break, usually made by the breakers but occasionally by Sergeant Collins and his machine, it was passed to the setters, whose job it was to extend that break until the entire set of wheel settings could be seen. Then they had to work out what the setting of the keys would be at the start of the message. Similar skills were required for both the breakers and the setters and most had passed through the training in cryptanalysis at Bedford. The jobs of breaker and setter were to a large extent interchangeable and there was fairly frequent movement of personnel between the two groups. But breaking, it was generally recognized, required a higher degree of skill than setting. Sometimes when the passing of "broken" dechis became too slow to keep the setters fully occupied, we from the setters section would get hold of some dechis and start to break as well as set them.

After the setters had identified the wheel settings at the beginning of a message, it was passed to the third section of the Testery where highly skilled and accurate typists typed in the utter nonsense of the encrypted message and out came clear military German. From there it was sent on to be translated and passed on to higher authorities including Winston Churchill himself.

The setters, of whom I was one, tended to be younger and less experienced than the breakers, but we were all trained cryptographers and we all had a good working knowledge of German, many of us being linguists. Most of us had just completd our first year at either Oxford or Cambridge University. There were a also a few older men, such as Ray Gardner, who was a Staff Sergeant in the Royal Army Education Corps when he was transferred to Bletchley. There were a few civilians working as breakers or setters, but there were no women. We were mostly NCOs though there were a few officers, such as Captain Maddocks and Captain Len Wesson and, for a while, Roy Jenkins. In fact the head of each shift of setters was normally a commissioned officer, but when the officer in charge of the setters on Peter Ericsson's shift was moved, Peter appointed me to be in charge. I was a 20 year-old Staff Sergeant in the Intelligence Corps at the time. Since then I have had many different jobs with much more high sounding titles and much higher pay, but I don't think I have ever had more real responsibility than I had then, when the work being done in the Testery affected the whole future of mankind. Thank God we did a good job.

Mu good friend Ray Gardner was senior to me in the rank of Staff Sergeant and was, not unnaturally somewhat hurt that he was passed over when a new head of the setters was chosen. I told him I understood how he must feel and how much I needed him and depended on him to help me do a good job. We remained firm friends and I knew I could always rely on him to give his best. I was very pleased when, after the war in Europe came to an end, Colonel Fillingham, who had been commandant of the army camp at Bletchley, was appointed to head one of the Formation Colleges that were set up to train people about to be demobilised with the skills they would need in civilian life, and he asked for Ray to be one of the instructors at the college. Ray left and was promoted to W.O. I.

Our expert typists worked on the so-called Tunny machines which emulated the German Lorenz machines on which the messages had been enciphered. These machines, designed, built and maintained by Post Office Research engineers were entirely electronic and contained hundreds of glass thermionic valves as well as hundreds of relays. Our engineers had accomplished an extraordinary feat by designing machines which emulated the functions of a machine they had never seen. They had had to work backwards, so to speak, to design machines that would copy exactly what the German machines did. Unlike Enigma no Lorenz machine was ever captured by the Allies until the end of the German war. When we first saw one we were amazed. It was not an electronic machine. It was in fact a rather compact machine incorporating a keyboard and it was entirely mechanical. Whereas the Testery's Tunny machines were six feet or more high, these German machines were little larger than a modern laser printer.

Those of us who did the work, as breakers, setters and typists did not get to see the clear German text when it was decoded and typed out. These clear language texts were whipped immediately away to be "processed" and the information was extracted and passed on to those who would use it. All we saw were the small bits we had worked on ourselves. There are just two bits that I still remember. One was included in a transmission that we had believed to be of great importance, but all it said was that Corporal Franks needed a new pair of boots. The other was a very unpleasant piece from Joseph Goebbels. It was about an anti-semitic pamphlet that had been found in the pockets of a dead US soldier's uniform. It began by asking questions such as "Who was the first American infrantryman to be awarded the Congressional Medal of Honor ?" or "Who was the first US airman to bring down a German bomber?" The answers to all the questions were given and they were all Irish names. The final question was "Who was the first son of a bitch to get four new tyres for his Cadillac ?" and the answer was "Nathan Cohen." Goebbels apparently felt that this nasty little pamphlet should be given the widest possible publicity.

Just as we seldom, if ever, saw the full extent of the information we passed on, we also seldom, if ever, received any feedback from the ultimate recipients of the strategical information contained in the transmissions. The one exception to this, that I remember, was a signal sent by General Marc Clark, who said that information we had sent him had prevented a division under his command from, so to speak, walking right into a trap set by the Germans. He commented that the information had saved thousands of allied soldiers lives.

After we had been in the Testery a few weeks, and we became more skilled in our work, promotions started coming our way; first one stripe making us Lance Corporals; then a second making us Corporals; then a third making us Sergeants. I was very proud of getting my third stripe on my 365th day of service in the army. That third stripe also radically affected my social life, as now I was a member of the Sergeants Mess. Your rank as an NCO indicated how long you had been working at Bletchley Park more than it did how well you did your work.

A reconstructed Tunny machine at the Bletchley Park Museum. It's working is being explained by Phil Hayes, Senior Colossus Engineer who worked with the late Tony Sales in bringing to life again the technology that played such an important role in the allied victory in Europe in World War II.

The teleprinter keyboard is just to the right of the electronic machinery that mimicked the working of the Lorenz machine, but did it electronically rather than mechanically. Contrast this machine with the actual Lorenz machine shown in the next picture.

An actual example of the German Lorenz SZ40 machine.
The twelve wheels can be clearly seen. The machine is mechanical and quite compact so that it could be loaded into a truck and moved from place to place; something that would have been extremely difficult with the electronic Tunny machine.

The author with the rebuilt Colossus, the world's first programmable electronic computer. Colossus was able to set the Chi keys of messages in Tunny. It was operated by Wrens in the Newmanry, under the eminent mathematician Max Newman and his team of mathematicians and cryptographers.

Colossus was designed and built by Tommy Flowers of the Post Office Research Station at Dollis Hill, but Flowers never received the recognition he deserved. In part this is due to the secrecy that surrounded the work at Bletchley on Tunny and was not lifted until the mid 1980s and partly because after the war Churchill ordered that all the various versions of Colossus except one were to be destroyed.

The Army Camp at Bletchley:
The Sergeants Mess

I don't think much has ever been written about the
army camp where members of the military wing of Government Communications Headquarters at Bletchley Park were
housed. The army camp and the neighboring RAF camp
were located right next to Bletchley Park itself. The army
camp housed the military personnel that worked in Bletchley
Park as well as the usual complement of support staff dealing with transportation, stores, medical services, etc.

The camp commandant was Lt.Col. G.S. Fillingham
whose previous posting had been as Commanding Officer
of a young soldiers battalion of the Durham Light Infantry,
and the Regimental Sergeant Major was RSM Conners.

The powers that were must have given a good deal
of thought in picking the men for these two posts as this
was no ordinary military camp. The majority of the men and

women stationed there were not the usual variety of soldiers; many of them were intellectuals, accomplished artists, musicians, and athletes. ; For example, I was once showing the wife of the Chairman of the Rural District Council around the camp and we came to the music hut - how many army camps, I wonder, had a music hut? - where a corporal was playing the piano. When we came out of the hut the chairman's wife exclaimed. "That corporal, 'e do play lovely." I had to explain to her that he was Corporal Wilfred Dunwell, professor of piano at one of the prestigious academies of music in London.

Both the army and the RAF camps were essentially self contained. In the army camp we had our own Medical Officer (M.O.), a young woman doctor, assisted by an elderly medical orderly, who was an old soldier. It was he who was in charge of one of the army's weirder practices, usually referred to as FFI, short for "free from infection."

Later the procedure's name was changed to HI or Health Inspection. Once a week we all had to form a long queue and one by one present ourselves to this rather grumpy old soldier exposing our genitals for his inspection. In theory this would enable him to ascertain whether we were suffering from any sexually transmitted disease or not. I believe the practice was eventually dropped.

Occasionally members of the army camp required treatment beyond what the young M.O. or her assistant could offer. Sometimes she could arrange for treatment to be given in the RAF camp which had rather more extensive medical facilities. For example, I had developed severe back pains and she arranged for me to receive massage therapy at the RAF camp.

On another occasion I caught mumps and had to be sent away to an army Camp Reception Station (CRS) staffed by nurses from Queen Alexandra's Nursing Corps (the army's official corps of nurses, all of whom were comissioned officers.)

The CRS was housed in a large private residence in Northampton and served all army units within a fairly large radius of that city. Another service that the RAF shared with us was the chaplaincy service. Squadron Leader Rev. Arthur Berey was the RAF padre, who became a good personal friend of mine. He made himself available to all army or RAF personnel and besides that he took a good deal of additional responsibility in the local Anglican parish, frequently taking the services in the Bletchley church and preaching the sermons. In fact the popularity of the services offered by Padre Berey, which drew much bigger congregations than those conducted by the vicar, an extremely dull and ineffectual man, eventually led to jealousy on the vicar's part and at one point he started making very derogatory remarks about the Rev. Berey from the pulpit. However, I think he was ignored by those who actually knew and liked the padre.

Clashes between the military culture and the very non-military Bletchley Park culture were mostly avoided due to the good sense displayed by both Fillingham and Conners. In one of the many books about Bletchley Park I have seen Fillingham described as having been considered somewhat mad and out of his depth in dealing with the assorted bunch of eccentrics in battle dress who worked in BP. Indeed he did have his own eccentricities, but perhaps that was why he was able, on the whole, to get on pretty well with those under his charge. It has to be admitted that to try to impose normal rigid military discipline on the Bletchley soldiers was an almost impossible task and in fairness to Fillingham he handled a difficult task rather well.

I can only remember one minor but amusing clash between the military and the Bletchley Park cultures. This occurred when a Lieutenant from the young soldiers battalion of the Durham Light Infantry came to the camp as Assistant Adjutant. He obviously had not been properly briefed. On one of his first mornings after arrival he was touring the camp with RSM Conners on a routine daily inspection and he came upon a bed with the blankets and kit laid out on it in proper army fashion, but he observed that there were none of the mandatory metal studs on the boots laid there.

"Sergeant Major, that man's on a charge. There are no studs on his boots."

"But sir," replied Conners, "That is RSM. Briggs' bed, sir." (Even in normal military establishments subalterns do not normally put soldiers of the rank of Regimental Sergeant Major on charges for minor offences.)

"I don't care who he is. That man is on a charge."

The young Lieutenant was due to go to Oxford after the war and it was later that day that he discovered he had just put the man who was due to become his tutor at his college on a charge for a very minor offence. Nor did he understand why he got such funny looks from fellow members of the Officers' Mess at lunch that day.

The Sergeants' Mess at Bletchley was, I think, quite

unique in the annals of the British army. I am sure there has never been another one quite like it.

RSM Conners of the Black Watch presided over the Mess, though there were a number of other W.O. Is of equal rank to Conners in the Mess. He was exactly the right man to be the Sergeant Major of the camp. He was a regular soldier among all of us war-time-only recruits. It was said that he had been educated at Dulwich College and that during his career he had been offered a commission but had preferred to stay in the ranks. He was equally at home with other regular soldiers and with the university faculty members and students that made up most of the membership of the Mess, including those of a rank equivalent to his own, such as W.O.1 Peter Benenson, who went on to become the Founder of Amnesty International and W.O.1 Asa Briggs who became the first head of the Open University in Britain.

Towards the end of the war when the general election was pending, Peter Benenson took leave so that he could act as the election agent for a young officer, also at Bletchley, whose name was Roy Jenkins, later Lord Jenkins. (Many years later when I went to Buckingham Palace to receive from Her Majesty Queen Elizabeth II the MBE that I had been awarded for work I had done in Nigeria, the Home Secretary reading out the names as we were called forward to stand in front of Her Majesty was the same man, Roy Jenkins, by then, like myself rather older.)

Other typical fellow members of the Mess that I remember included Sgt. Herbert Murrill, later Director of Music at the BBC. Tragically Murrill died quite young. But while at Bletchley he was able to invite another composer friend of his, Sgt. Edmund Rubbra, who was head of the army classical music group, to give a concert in the Mess. We were not starved for good music at Bletchley, that's for sure! One of the members of the Mess was the brother-in-law of Reg Kilbey, cellist from the Albert Sandler Trio, a very popular broadcasting group at the time. Kilbey, accompanied by Jack Byfield, the Trio's pianist, came several times to play for us, but there was also plentiful musical talent within the membership of the mess itself.

Among the women members, Sergeant Jeanne Cammaerts is one who stands out in my mind. She was the daughter of the Belgian intellectual Emile Cammaerts, and I think English was probably not her first language. She was a big and imposing young woman and she showed considerable acting talent as Eliza Doolittle in a production of Shaw's Pygmalion with the parts of Professor Higgins and Colonel Pickering played by fellow members of the Sergeants' Mess. Another woman sergeant went on to become the editor of one of the leading women's magazines in Britain.

Others members of the mess included Leo Jolley who joined the central office of the Labour Party after the war and became, I believe, the general secretary of the party. Also I remember with affection a Sergeant who came from the Channel Islands, Eric de Carteret. He loved to dance, but only with girls who were taller than he was.

Although normal military discipline was enforced inside the camp, this was not so within Bletchley Park itself. There was no saluting. We were all colleagues working towards a common goal. Our responsibilities varied and, of course, there were some people in managerial and supervisory positions as in any large organization, but those responsibilities did not always correspond to relative military ranks. In my own case, as a Staff Sergeant I was the supervisor of one of the three shifts of setters in the Testery. Of the other two shifts, one had a Captain (Len Wesson) in charge and the other was headed by a civilian with a Captain as his second in command. And from time to time I had commissioned officers working in the section that I supervised. This was not a problem. Everyone worked well together for the greater good of our work, and a general ssense of cameraderie prevailed.

This apparent paradox was most clearly illustrated when Staff Sergeant Singleton, in civilian life a senior civil servant in the Ministry of Labour, was posted away from Bletchley Park as the war with Germany was ending. He was needed to take charge of labor problems in Germany after the war. For this task he was, we heard, given the rank of Brigadier. From three stripes and a crown on your arm to three pips and a crown on your shoulder is quite a jump and it was, I imagine, the most exceptional promotion in the British army in World War II.

Social Life of a Code Breaker

Becoming a member of the Testery at Bletchley Park opened up a whole new social life for me. The people I worked with directly became my close friends. Most of us got bicycles, so that we could get around easily, as there was no public transport in Bletchley, although Bletchley Junction railway station was only a short walk from the army camp. Those of us who had trained at Bedford and were now working as setters in the Testery were all male, but the typists who took over after we had worked out the wheel settings for each transmission were mostly young women. Naturally we tended to divide up into pairs. My Welsh friend, Dai Rees, paired off with a very attractive girl named Bobby Roberts. I paired off with her best friend, a Scottish girl named Babs.

Some nearby gravel pits provided natural swimming pools where we all spent time when the weather allowed. Sometimes I went cycling with one or other of the group. I remember going for long cycle trips with Tom Mashiter, who had a serious speech defect, a terrible stutter that he could not control. There was very little motor traffic on the roads because of petrol rationing, and that made cycling much easier and pleasanter. Sometimes groups of us organized by W.O.II Helen Pollard (now Currie) would go to theater performances in Northampton. She would always manage to organize a truck to take us there and bring us back ro camp. Northampton had two theaters, a variety theater and a repertory theater. I will always remember the thrill of seeing Richard Tauber playing the leading role in one of the operettas he had written himself, called "Old Chelsea." Although he was past his prime, he still had a remarkably good voice.

But my social life changed considerably after I was promoted to Sergeant and became a member of the Sergeants Mess.

There were two aspects to the social life of those working in Bletchley Park. One was the social side of life in the Park and in the army camp. One thing I have never seen mentioned in any article or book about BP was the fact that there were a number of very competent sports men and women working there. For example a young officer named David Warwick had been the winner of the junior men's singles at Wimbledon. Who knows how far he might have gone in his tennis career if it had not been for the war. Some years later I was at Wimbledon watching from the cheap unreserved seats around the Central court. I don't remember who was playing, but I recognized one of the line judges. It was David Warwick.

Also there was a Jewish NCO, whose name was (I think) Sidney Levy. It was said that he had been runner-up in the World Table Tennis championships. I myself was a fairly good pingpong player and I quite often played (and won against) one of our male typists, who played for his county. The ping pong tables were actually in the Mansion itself and I would often play a few games with one of my fellow setters before going on a nightshift. The concentration involved in playing table tennis helped to sharpen one's wits for the concentration needed to do the work on Tunny.

The other two sports in which I participated were boxing and middle to long distance running. In the hut where I lived (before I got my own tiny room in huts reserved for senior NCOs.) one of the camp maintenance soldiers was Gunner Avis, who had been boxing instructor for the Metropolitan Police. He took me under his wing and gave me training sessions in the hut, no doubt much to the amusement of other members of the hut. Avis was a very big man and very tough. He looked like the professional pug that he was, but he always treated me well, pushing me mentally and physically but never really hurting me when we sparred together. I am sure he could have knocked me out in three minutes if he had had a mind to. When a travelling fair came to a place near Bletchley, he went and took temporary part time employment in the boxing booth. Potential boxers were challenged to stay in the ring with him for three minutes. I don't know how many made it, but I would imagine not too many.

As a member of the unit's boxing team I was entitled to double rations, but I quit the team after an incident, which occurred when our heavyweight, a young lieutenant, in civvy street a school master at Oundle, got into the ring with an opponent from another unit, and was almost immediately knocked out. He had not been told that the corporal from the other unit who was his opponent was the

36

amateur heavyweight champion of Great Britain. That was often the problem; you did not know the caliber of the athlete against whom you were competing,

We had two brothers in the camp both of whom were serious runners. We all used to train regularly on the Buckinghamshire Education Committee's athletic grounds. Roy Booker was a much better runner than I was but we used to run together on the Bucks track.. The grounds were not big enough to allow for a normal 440 yard track, which gives four laps to the mile. So they had created a five-laps-to-the-mile track. Also the ground was on a distinct slope – not exactly an ideal track by any means.

On one occasion our athletics team was drawn to take on the Army Pay Corps team, but this time we were given the names of our opponents. I saw that my opponent in the mile was to be Corporal Sidney Wooderson. I decided that my duties would prevent me from taking part that day for the fact was that Sidney Wooderson was a world famous athlete; winner of the gold medal in the pre-war Olympics, and current holder of the world record for the mile run.

Few people working in BP had much contact with the townspeople of Bletchley. I was one of the few who had a great deal of contact with them, and this was due to meeting a petite Sergeant, named Joan Chandler, to whom I referred earlier and who was to play such an important role in my life for the next two years. What brought about our getting together in the first place was that we both belonged to a movement known, by the rather off-putting name, of Moral ReArmament (MRA.) (Mind you it had previously been known as the Oxford Group and as a Cambridge man

I would never have been willing to be called an "Oxford Grouper.") Joan had noticed that in my mail pigeon hole in the Sergeants Mess I was getting copies of an MRA newsletter. So she contacted me and we met. She told me that there was a small MRA group at Bletchley which met regularly. The other two members of the group were a widow, Elsie Sisk, who was a telephone operator in the Park, and the Reverend Arthur Berey, the RAF padre. The group met regularly in his office in the RAF camp..

Despite its unfortunate name MRA was in fact a most exciting movement. Its activities in both the U.K. and the U.S.A. were, to a considerable extent, concerned with problems of national morale, that both countries needed to deal with if the war against Nazism was to be won. The U.K. branch of MRA had produced a colorful, red, white and blue pamphlet called "Battle Together for Britain" and hoped to get copies into every home in Britain. (In the U.S. there was an analogous pamphlet called "You Can Defend America.")

In the small team of which I now became a member, we undertook to get copies distributed throughout the Bletchley and neighboring Fenny Stratford area. But first we had to overcome a few problems; we had no funds to buy the copies for distribution and we had no means of distributing them, even if we were able to buy them.

The four of us, Arthur Berey, Elsie Sisk, Joan and I, planned our strategy together at our regular meetings in the Padre's office in the RAF camp, but the actual leg work fell to Joan and me as the two younger members of the group. So we got on our bikes, rode into the town and started

38

knocking on doors. In this way we came to meet the Chairman of the Rural District Council, Syd Maycock, a railway guard. Syd and his wife became great friends of ours. Mrs Maycock was rather stout and had a pronounced limp wearing a heavy surgical boot on one foot. Joan and I often sat down to tea with them and we enjoyed the wonderful fruit cake that Syd's wife managed to make from their war time rations.

We also made friends with the staff of the two local weekly newspapers, the *Bletchley Gazette* and the *North Bucks Chronicle*. My first published poem, which looked at Bletchley as a transport gateway where trunk roads, mainline railway and the canal system all met, was published in the *Bletchley Gazette*. The poem could not, of course, refer to the most important aspect of the place at that time, i.e. its location as the center of one of the Allies' most important secret activities of the war.

We held several public meetings in a hall in the town. To help us with these a friend, Staff Quarter Master Sergeant (SQMS) Bob Riddell of the Royal Army Ordnance Corps would come down from London. I could always find a place for him to stay in the senior NCOs' quarters and he would join us for meals in the Sergeants Mess.

Bob was a great ally and a great friend. He persuaded me to sing some patriotic songs of those days accompanied by a rather proper local pianist and I'd like to think that was not the main reason that our public meetings were rather sparsely attended! They were however fully reported in our two local newspapers though they sometimes got our names slightly wrong. On one occasion instead of calling me Staff

Sergeant Mayo-Smith, they promoted me and I became Staff Sergeant Major Smith.

Additionally Joan and I met and made friends with two families, the Coxes and the Harlocks. Mr Cox and Mr Harlock were in charge of the Boy Scouts in the area. They also become good friends on whom we could drop in any time we were in the town.

Finally we were introduced to a man who owned a local factory, though to this day I do not know what it made. Perhaps his work was just as secret as ours. We visited him at his home and he listened to us after offering us each a glass of port. Although at that time neither Joan nor I would normally touch alcohol we accepted out of politeness. After hearing what we had to say he offered to pay the whole cost of the booklets.

That evening I remember walking back to the camp with Joan. My feet did not touch the ground. I was walking on air. Everything was going so well and I was with Joan. As you have probably guessed, by this time I was head over heels in love with this wonderful young woman. She was four years older than me and ten times more mature. She was a leader I was extremely happy to follow. We became very close and could often be seen walking with our arms around each others' waists. It must have been quite a sight as she was under five feet tall and I was a good six foot four in my army boots.

After we had secured the funds for the booklets we talked to Messrs Cox and Harlock and they arranged to get the boy scouts to distribute them in every home in Bletchley and neighboring Fenny Stratford.

So with the help of all the friends we had made in the town we achieved what I had a first thought impossible. I felt (and still feel) almost as proud of this achievement as I was of the critically important work we were doing as cipher breakers inside the Park.

When the end of the war in Europe came on VE day, Joan and I went up to London and joined the huge throng of people outside Buckingham Palace. Eventually the King and Queen came out on the balcony and waved to the crowd of thousands of us gathered there. It was a day to be remembered and treasured always.

There was one other event that took many members of the Testery outside the grounds of BP. This was the general election held towards the end of the war. Young Captain Roy Jenkins was standing as a Labour Party candidate for one of the Northern constituencies. He, of course, was given leave to conduct this campaign. His campaign manager was RSM Peter Benenson. Several other members of the Testery took whatever leave was due to them to go and work on Roy's campaign. Roy lost, but a good time was had by all. Not long afterwards Roy did get into Parliament, winning a seat in a bye election. So began his highly successful political career.

As you would expect in a large organization in which hundreds of men, mostly young and many of them single worked together with hundreds of young women, who were also mostly young and single, there were many romances. And love it seems is no respecter of rank, so there were quite a number of cases in which an officer in one of the armed forces fell in love with a ranker. Sometimes it was the husband who was the officer but sometimes it was the wife. My friend Freddie Snewin, an officer in the WAAF was engaged to a man in the ranks. In this situation it was impossible for husband and wife to take their meals together in the Mess, and technically one partner should have had to salute the other whenever they met. Most of the people I knew who were in this situation viewed it with a mixture of amusement and minor irritation.

There were plenty of romances and marriages across service lines. Another friend Derrick Langford, who was an army Corporal in the Testery married a WREN from the Newmanry, though the wedding did not actually take place until Derrick was back at Cambridge. It was a quiet wedding. I was best man and all the guests were former members of either the Testery or the Newmanry.

One wedding did caused quite a stir in the army camp. The bride, a rather upper class ATS girl went AWOL and was missing for two days. Then she came back to camp wreathed in smiles. She told everyone willing to listen how she had run away to get married. She was an aspiring actress and the bridegroom was a theatrical producer. She described the wedding itself in detail and then she added "Of course, it's purely a marriage of convenience. He can help me in my career and I can help him by acting as his hostess."

Ray Gardner, another Testery friend was a former school teacher and came to us on transfer from the Royal Army Education Corps. He was able to bring his wife with him and they lived together in digs in Leighton Buzzard, one station on the railway line from Bletchley Junction. Ray was a Methodist lay preacher and took an active part in the life of the Leighton Buzzard Methodist Church.

In addition to those romances that ended happily there were affairs that ended unhappily. For example a married major in the Testery had an affair with an ATS officer (not in the Testery) and she became not only pregnant but mentally disturbed by the situation. I do not know how this problem was eventually dealt with.

If you are wondering what happened to Joan and me, I can only tell you that she was demobilized some time before I was and she went to work as a full time volunteer for Moral ReArmament. Joan had a confidante and mentor in the London headquarters of MRA, and I don't think she approved of me. I believe she advised Joan to distance herself from me for the foreseeable future. I did however, propose to Joan more than once, but she always turned me down. She was four years older than me and, as I have already said, ten times more mature and maybe she was right to turn me down - but I'll never really believe that!

Anyway after Bletchley I returned to Cambridge from where I graduated and I accepted an assignment as an Intelligence Office with the British Military Mission to Greece and to my regret I lost touch with this woman who was my best friend and who had meant so much to me. Years later when I finally did try to get back in touch, I learned that she had died of cancer.

Bletchley Park People
The Three Main Categories

To my mind the various people involved in decoding secret encoded messages at Bletchley Park could be roughly divided into three categories; mathematicians, crossword puzzlers and engineers. Those in each category were backed up by well trained support staff. The mathematicians and the engineers were mostly civilians and the crossword puzzlers were mostly military. The very large support staff were mostly in the uniform of one of the three armed services.

The engineers designed, built and maintained the machines. The mathematicians provided the theoretical base on which the machines were built. The crossword puzzlers took the product of the machines and managed to make enough sense of it to enable the next lot of machines to be set up to decode the messages. At least that's how it worked in the Testery.

If you can imagine a puzzle that was a cross between an advanced Sudoku puzzle and the Daily Telegraph (or The Times) cryptic crossword puzzle written in military German, then you have some idea what it was like breaking Tunny. First you had to have someone who could figure out how these very complex puzzles were constructed. For Tunny this was Bill Tutte, who somehow worked out the structure of Tunny. Today it still seems to me an almost incredible achievement, though Tutte received little recognition for his brilliant work.

Then it took another genius, the Post Office Research engineer, Tommy Flowers, to design and build a machine which could do the first part of decoding messages sent in the Tunny cipher. In turn his work would not have been possible without the brilliant theoretical work done by mathematical genius Alan Turing.

Flowers, later in his life received some recognition for the work he did in automating Britain's telephone system, but he received scant recognition for building Colossus, the world's first ever electronic computer. He and his colleagues also built the Tunny machines which emulated the working of the German Lorenz machines. Flower's machines were electronic, and the German machines were mechanical, but they did the job of decoding perfectly, though they took up rather more space than the German machines. Examples of both machines can now be seen at the National Museum of Computing, which is also situated in Bletchley Park.

As for Turing, far from rewarding him for his huge contributions to the Allied war effort, he was hounded by the authorities because of his homosexuality and it drove him to suicide.

In the Testery's sister section, the Newmanry, the mathematicians ruled the roost They were headed by Max

Newman, and included Donald Michie who also worked in the Testery. Their support staff included the engineers who maintained the machines and the Wrens who operated the various versions of Colossus.

In the Testery it was mainly the crossword puzzlers who ruled. Both the setters and the breakers had in essence to be able to do crossword puzzles in military German. Most had been recruited from Cambridge, Oxford and London Universities. In the setters' room, of which I came to be in charge, I can only think of one person who was not either an Oxford or Cambridge undergraduate. The exception was Ray Gardner a Staff Sergeant who came to us from the Army Education Corps. Most of us wore the khaki battle dress of the army, though there were a few civilians as well.

On Captain Peter Ericsson's shift in the Testery, the breakers and setters were all male and most were in the army. To the best of my memory no women were employed as either a breaker or setter in the Testery.

I don't know whether Ray Gardner had gone through the training at the cipher school in Bedford, but all the rest of us had. Dai Rees, the Welshman, who used to lead us in singing comic songs while we worked, was from Oxford, but the majority of my shift of setters, as far as I can remember, were all from Cambridge.

My friends and colleagues at Bletchley were a great bunch to work with. Chick Philps had a soft West Country accent and had some skill as an artist. He was eventually commissioned. Tom Mashiter had a serious speech impediment and stuttered terribly. John Dent and John Nash had both been brought up by their mothers who had been widowed early. The difference their upbringing had made showed up in various small ways.

Our shift's support staff consisted of a few male army typists from the Royal Army Service Corps and a group of attractive young girls from the Auxiliary Territorial Service (ATS), the women's branch of the British army. They were supervised by ATS officers.

I cannot say anything about the staffing of other sections at Bletchley. Although there was a large RAF camp for the members of the Royal Air Force working at BP we did not intermingle with them very much. There was some dating between the Wrens in the Newmanry with male members of the Testery but this was hampered by the fact that the Wrens were billeted some distance away from Bletchley and were bussed in every day for their shifts.

When I try to think of people at Bletchley Park who were close friends I can think of only a handful who were not in the army. I had one friend, Hugh Wilkinson, who was a Royal Navy Volunteer Reserve, Sub Lieutenant, but I had known him before he came to Bletchley. He had worked in the Japanese Naval Section, though I do not know what kind of work he was doing. We were both back at Cambridge after the war and after graduating he went to live in Japan and has remained there ever since. We still correspond with each other.

In the RAF camp, the only person I knew really well on a personal level was the padre, Rev. Arthuer Berey. I did have to go to the RAF camp at one time for physical therapy which was not available in the army camp and I got to know the Leading Aircraftman who gave me shoulder massages.

Disbanding of the Testery and the Move to Eastcote

From D Day until the end of the war with Germany the Testery was working flat out. The information that came from the breaking of Tunny messages leading up to D Day were of tremendous significance, as they resulted in the Commander-in-Chief of the Allied Forces in Europe, General Eisenhower being in full possession of the location of all Hitler's forces before the Allied landings. He commented afterwards that the information he had received   resulted in cutting the war shorter by two years. Literally hundred of thousands of lives on both sides were saved. But after VE Day, when the war in Europe ended, there were no more Tunny messages to decipher, and there was no further need for a Testery.

Before the Testery was disbanded we were able to see a captured Lorenz machine and, as I remarked earlier, we were dumbstruck to see how small this entirely mechanical machine was when compared to the Tunny machines used in the Testery for the final decrypting of the messages.

A Lorenz SZ40 cipher machine on display at Bletchley Park.
The twelve notched wheels that produced the twelve keys of Tunny (5 chi
keys, 5 psi keys and 2 motor keys) can be clealy seen.

We were amazed at the relatively small size of the German
machine, as compared to the 6 foot high electronic Tunny machines that were
developed to decipher the messages.

So there we were, trained as cryptographers and familiar with the complexities of Tunny messages but now with nothing to do! That situation did not last for long however. A few of us, including Corporal Derrick Langford, and, if I remember rightly, Sergeant Dai Rees, were told to learn the Serbo-Croat language. We were not sure what we were going to do with it after we had learnt it. I speculated that possibly we were going to be parachuted into Yugoslavia to join Brigadier Fitzroy MacLean, who was head of the British liaison team with Marshal Tito. But it turned out that our next task was to be somewhat less exciting. Anyway we were taught the language and soon were fluent enough to be given our next assignment which was to break the coded messages of OZNA, the Yugoslav secret police equivalent of the KGB in Russia.

This is when the training we had received in Bedford really came to our aid. The OZNA messages were in a manual, rather than a machine generated cipher. I cannot now recall the exact form of this cipher but it was one of those ciphers in which any two consecutive letters were enciphered together giving you a different two letter group.

We didn't have too much difficulty in solving these messages daily. Some of the messages were very short, just two words, "Liquidate" followed by a name.

Once I almost made a horrible howler. In early January a whole lot of messages came through in which, instead of the usual signatories' names at the end of the message they all ended with the words Srecan Bozic. Now Srecan is a genuine Serbian forename and Bozic is a genuine surname. I began to think that there must have been a huge change in the Yugoslav political hierarchy with someone called Srecan Bozic rising to the top. I told Derrick of this remarkable discovery. Fortunately for me before I passed this news higher up the line I remembered what time of year it was. The Orthodox Christmas, celebrated in Serbia, fell on January 6. Srecan means "Happy" and "Bozic" translates as "Christmas." The messages had in fact just been ending in Christmas greetings.

Another time I was able to break a message because it included the Serbo-Croat word for maize. "kukuruz." The unusual pattern created by this word gave me the help I needed to decipher the message.

About this time the activities at Bletchley Park were moved to new offices at Eastcote, and the army camp was moved to Latimer, quite close to the Chalfont and Latimer underground railway station. We then became uniformed commuters traveling each morning from the camp to the offices in Eastcote. There were no more night or evening shifts. We had become just a crowd of office workers. Of course we were still in touch at Eastcote with others we had known at Bletchley.

On one occasion that sticks out in my mind as being memorable I was asked to take one of the civilian girls to a dance. Freddie worked in another section, and had previously been asked by a Sergeant, named Peter, to go with him to this dance, but at the last minute he had copped out as he had become attracted to another girl and had asked her instead, just unfeelingly dumping Freddie.

Freddie was very well liked by my friends, though I don't think I had met her, and they wanted to show their disapproval of Peter's behavior by arranging things so that he would see Freddie at the dance with another man and feel ashamed of his callous dropping of her.

Freddie came from the East End of London, the poorest area. Her face bore pox marks. But she was a lively, vivacious person and great fun to be with. I immediately liked her. I found her to be extremely attractive and had it not been for the fact that I was deeply in love with Joan (who had since been demobilized) I would very happily have taken up with Freddie on a more permanent basis. She made such a deep impression on me that I have never forgotten her, even though I only spent that one evening at the dance with her.

Derrick and I shared our office at Eastcote with a lady who dealt with Hungarian ciphers and a man named Griffenhagen who dealt with Rumanian army traffic. It was a rather amusing situation as the lady, who had great admiration for the Hungarians, had nothing but contempt for Rumanians and frequently expressed her opinions of them.

One day I was handed a Rumanian Dictionary and told to get myself familiar with the language as I was to take over part of the Rumanian traffic. The Rumanian language is a Latin based language and incorporates many Slav words plus some Turkish or Arabic words. Without being able really to speak it, it was nevertheless easy to understand the written language. The Rumanian dictionary, however, was not a lot of help . I sometimes wondered how it ever came to be published, as the authors did not appear to have too great a knowledge of English. At the end of the book there was a collection of "English Proverbs and Idioticisms." That was probably a more accurate description than the authors had meant it to be, for it did not have much information on English idioms but there were plenty of idioticisms. One of the ones I remember should have read "The rolling stone gathers no moss." but instead it read "The stone as roll heap up no foam."

The Rumanian army traffic for which I became responsible used a form of cipher rather similar to the Yugoslav OZNA traffic. The Rumanians made it incredibly easy to break their messages because they started every single communication with the words (in Rumanian, of course) "I have the honor to report to you that…...." Knowing exactly what the first few words of each message were, made it a piece of cake to decipher the rest of the message.

Eventually I received a Class B release from the army which allowed me to be demobilized and return to Cambridge with an adequate grant to cover my fees and living expenses for the next two years.

A number of my colleagues followed me back to Cambridge and so we stayed in touch with each other. Derrick and I both decided to continue our studies of Serbo-Croat and the history and culture of the southern Slavs. We were joined by John Dening who had been an Intelligence Corps Captain and had also learned Serbo-Croat at Bletchley.

I dropped German and instead took Russian as my other language. I remember telling my former German supervisor that German would cease to be a language of any great importance after their defeat in the war and that Russian was to become the important language in which to be fluent. Of course I could not have been more wrong about the importance of the German language and I am very glad that I never quite lost my German as one of my passions in life is Viennese operetta.

For a while I shared rooms at my College, Clare, with a former member of the Testery, Captain John Dening, who had been, if I remember rightly, a fellow setter.

Dai Rees went back to Oxford and I saw him once more when a group of us, driven by Professor (later Dame) Elizabeth Hill in her tiny Fiat Topolino car, went to Oxford to study at first hand a copy of Dusan's code, which provided the foundation of the laws of the southern Slavs.

I even studied Medieval Serbian and learnt old Serbian songs. On one occasion Derrick and I and two fellow students of Medieval Serbian sang a selection of them as a warm up act for a Russian bass who was giving a concert to the Slavonic Society at Cambridge. The pianist who accompanied us was another friend from BP, former Sub-lieutenant Hugh Wilkinson, RNVR, who had been working on Japanese naval codes.

When, as already mentioned, Derrick married his former Wren fiancee nearly all the male guests at this quiet wedding were former army personnel from the Testery. Most of the female guests were from the Newmanry.

Eventually we all graduated and moved on.

One of my last acts at Cambridge was to visit Addenbrooke's Hospital to say "Goodbye" to one of my best friends from those days, "Chick" Philps. He was suffering from one of the childhood diseases, I think it was chicken pox. Although we all called him "Chick" Philps, his first names were actually Harold Daniel. He had a pleasant West Country accent. We had joined the Testery about the same time and had risen up the ranks together until he was selected for officer training. As a result he did not get back to Cambridge until a year later than I did. He left the army with, I think, the rank of Captain.

Years later I tried to get in touch with Joan and other old friends but the fact that our war time work still had to be kept secret for so long made it difficult for us to keep in touch with each other, and my subsequent career took me to many different parts of the world which did not help matters.

THE GOVERNMENT CODE
AND CYPHER SCHOOL

Ian Mayo-Smith

The Government wishes to express
to you its deepest gratitude
for the vital service you performed
during World War II

Rt Hon Gordon Brown MP
Prime Minister

July 2009

Welcome, if a trifle late, recognition for the work done by those who worked at Bletchley Park and its outstations during World War II. This certificate, signed by then Prime Minister Gordon Brown, was sent to all known survivors in June 2009. It was accompanied by the medallion shown in the photo on the next page.

Pleased as we were to receive these tokens of recognition of our contributions we could not help thinking of our comrades who had died without ever having been recognized for their war time work at BP or ever being able to tell their families about it.

56

An enlarged photo of the medallion sent to all Bletchley Park survivors in 2009. (Its actual diameter is approximately an inch and a half.) The letters GC&CS appear at the top and the wording at the bottom is "Bletchley Park and its outstations." Below the central blue stone are the dates 1939-1945.

Epilogue

It was a chilly and rather dull mid-November morning. My wife and I got out of the train at Bletchley and made our way to the entrance of Bletchley Park. We were to meet Joan's daughter, Jane, with whom I had managed to get in touch and with whom I had corresponded. When we went in to the entrance office of the Park a lady stepped forward and introduced herself. She had recognized us from a description I had emailed her. Her husband Peter and daughter Catie were with her. Before this we had only talked on the phone and exchanged emails, but had never met.

Since the embargo on talking or writing anything about what went on at Bletchley Park in World War II had not been lifted at the time of Joan's death, she had never been able to tell her two daughters about what she had done in those war-time years. Jane was most keen to learn more about this part of her mother's life. I had been able to tell her a certain amount in emails, but finally we were going to see the place where her mother had been part of this vital work.

In front of the mansion at Bletchley Park.

The author (center) and his wife Krishna with Jane Hayward and her husband Peter and daughter Catherine.

Jane Hayward is the daughter of the late Joan Chandler Allander, who played such an important part in the author's life during the time they were both in the army, working in Bletchley Park.

Guided tours were available and the five of us decided to take one which was just about to start. It was a good decision. Personally I learnt about some of the things that went on at BP, which I had not known. In addition all sorts of old memories came flooding back to me. I mentioned to the guide that I had worked at Bletchley as a soldier during the war, and at one point he told the group that I had worked on the Lorenz cipher, the most advanced cipher broken in World War II. There are not a lot of us left who had worked at Bletchley in those heady days, and I found I had become something of a center of interest.

Fellow members of the guided tour started asking if they could take my picture. A man taking the tour with his small son came up to me and told me that his son was tremendously interested in codes and ciphers. Would I mind if he took a photo of his son and me together? I began to wonder whether I was a visitor on the tour or an exhibit!

Later I was introduced to members of the group, many of them volunteers, who are preserving for posterity this place that played such a vital role in WWII. I was told that I was one of the very few known survivors who had worked in the "Testery" on the Lorenz cipher. One other being Captain Jerry Roberts with whom I later got in touch and finally met in London - after 65 years. The staff at BP suggested that I should write my memoirs of my work in the Testery at BP.

Afterwards I thought this would genuinely be a good idea and since I was going off for my annual winter pilgrimage to Thailand I would have plenty of time on my hands to do it. But where should I begin? I suppose it should be at the beginning and I could start by describing how an 18-year-old undergraduate reading French and German at Cambridge became an Intelligence Corps N.C.O. and a member of the team that daily broke the most advanced cipher messages (in the Lorenz cipher) to be broken during World War II.

Two old men reminiscing about their work in the Testery during World War II.

Captain Jerry Roberts (left) and the author, former Staff Sergeant Ian Mayo-Smith.

Jerry Roberts was head of one of the three shifts in the Testery and one of the senior cryptographers in the section from its beginning. The author came to the Testery later and became head of the setters on Captain Peter Ericsson's shift.

Further Reading

For further information about Tunny and the work of the Testery and Newmanry, the best possible source is the book **"Colossus,"** edited and co-written by Professor Jack Copeland and published by Oxford University Press.

In recent years many books have been written about Bletchley Park and the war-time work done there. They include the following:

Codebreakers, edited by Sir Harry Hinsley and Alan Strip, also published by Oxford Univeristy Press.

The Secret War by Michael Paterson, published by David & Charles.

The Secrets of Station X by Michael Smith, published by Biteback Publishing Ltd. This book goes back to the prewar roots of the organisation that eventually became known as the Government Codes and Cipher School It is available in printed form or as an e-book. The other titles mentioned may also be available in e-book form.

Those more interested in the Enigma cipher will

find **Dilly, The Man Who Broke Enigma** by Mavis Batey of interest. It is published by Biteback Publishing Ltd.

Simon Singh's history of codes and code-breaking, **The Code Book** (published by The Fourth Estate) includes several chapters about the work at Bletchley.

Anyone can become a friend of Bletchley Park for a small subscription and receive regular news letters about events at the Park, which has become one of Britain's most interesting museums. But if you have never been to the Park you should do so and visit the shop there where you can buy books and all sorts of memorabilia from the Park,

Also at Bletchley Park is the National Museum of Computing. Among the many items of interest there you will find the rebuilt Colossus, the world's first electronic computer as well as the Tunny machine and the German Lorenz machine.

About the Author

Dr. Ian Mayo-Smith is an Emeritus Professor of the University of Connecticut, and former Director of the Institute of Public Service International. Before joining the University in 1973 his career had taken him to many parts of the world.

He served in the Intelligence Corps in the British army from 1943 to 1946, during which period he worked in the Testery at Bletchley Park. After graduating from Cambridge University with a degree in French, Russian and Serbo-Croat, he worked as an Intelligence Officer with the British Military Mission to Greece from 1948 to 1952. This was followed by a year and a half of dreary work in the War Office. Then he took advantage of a transfer to the former Colonial Service and was sent to work in "Establishments" (i.e. personnel management) in the Government of the Northern Region of Nigeria. He stayed on after Nigerian Independence and after leaving the Civil Service he returned as a Ford Foundation "advisor." For his work in Nigeria he was awarded the M.B.E. by Her Majesty, Queen Elizabeth.

He then took a year off to go back to Cambridge, after which he took another Ford Foundation assignment, this time in Kenya, where he met and married Krishna Sondhi, a Kenyan of Punjabi origin, the highest ranking woman in the Kenya Civil Service, of whom he was somewhat in awe. (He still is.)

After four years in Kenya he was recruited by the University of Connecticut and moved to the U.S.A. of which he eventually became a citizen. His time at the University was interrupted for two years when he took an assignment with the United Nations in Arusha, Tanzania, where at that time the offices of the short lived East African Community were located. He claims that his greatest achievement at that time was the production of a musical review for which he co-wrote both the words and music, and which he directed and acted in. It was the first production that had ever been put on at the Little Theater in Arusha which had a completely multi-national, multi-racial, and multi-ethnic cast.

He finally retired from the University of Connecticut in 1988, becoming an Emeritus Professor. Harvard University then recruited him for work in Brunei where for two years he was the resident representative of the Harvard Institute for International Development and was engaged in the reform of the Brunei civil service.

After that he continued to do consulting work, mostly at the International Training Center of the I.L.O. in Turin, until his 70th birthday.

Since then he has tried to live the life of the idle rich, the only snag being that he is not rich and he is not very good at staying idle. However for several months each year he does manage to get closer to this ideal, as he and his wife, Krishna, spend the winter months in Thailand, where they have leased a home from a friend that Ian made there. His work for the University of Connecticut had taken him to Thailand for several weeks each year for seven years. He and his wife Krishna have become a part of the Thai family they stay with.

At his present age of 88 he still finds life worth living and has plenty to do. He is turning out books at the rate of about one a year. And he still remembers those wonderful years when he was a part of an extraordinary team of gifted men and women at Bletchley Park.

More from
Four Pillars Media Group

If you enjoyed **Eavesdropping on Adolf Hitler** you may enjoy **The Spyder's Web,** Ian Mayo-Smith's tongue in the cheek spy novel with the action taking place in a fictional South East Asian country. Although all the persons and places in the story are entirely fictitious, some of the events described in it are loosely based on Ian's experiences in British military intelligence as a young man in the postwar years. But the actions in the book reflect the world we live in today in which acts of terrorism are in the news with frightening frequency. The book will make you laugh but the plot will keep your attention as the suspense grows until the final denoument. Available now from Four Pillars Media Group (FPMG)..

Other books by Ian Mayo-Smith available from FPMG include
PEACE - Poems, Essays And Comments for Everyone,
and
Trying to Walk the Way
Both these books are collections of Ian's poetry and essays on contemporary issues.

The Children's Aviary

A little book about some rather unusual birds, such as the Messy Nester Hawk, the YakYak, and the Humphus Pumphus, delightfully illustrated by Andrea Doty. For children of all ages.

Positive People

co-written with Catherine Wyatt-Morley.

Catherine was a faithful wife and mother of three children, when she learnt that her unfaithful husband had infected her with the HIV virus. She lost her job and even her priest turned against her but she is a woman with an indomitable spirit. She went on to found a major organization (WOMEN) offering education and help to others infected with or affected by this dread disease. You may have heard Catherine on national television, but watch out for her latest book

My Life with AIDS: From Tragedy to Triumph

available from FPMG.

The Crumbling Empire

by Brian Walsh and Maura Satchell.

Imagine a child-molesting Catholic priest becoming the Pope. What would you do if you had been one of that monster's innocent victims? Read how victim Ben Clancy deals with the situation in this dramatic thriller.

Available in print or as an e-book for the Nook or Kindle.

Watch too for the sequel entitled
The Song of Revolution
which FPMG will also be bringing out in the near future..

All these books can be obtained direct from
Four Pillars Media Group,
P. O. Box 499, Meriden, CT 06450.
www.fourpillarsmediagroup.com

as well as:
Amazon.Com

Made in the USA
Las Vegas, NV
01 September 2021

29378614R00046